True
to Minimalism

A lifestyle that uses Multipurpose items

CAREY HARRIS

Copyright © 2019 by Carey Harris.

All rights reserved. No part of this publication may be reproduced, distributed or transmitted in any form or by any means, including photocopying, recording, or other electronic or mechanical methods, without the prior written permission of the publisher, except in the case of brief quotations embodied in critical reviews and certain other noncommercial uses permitted by copyright law. For permission requests, write to the publisher, at the address below.

Carey Harris

620 McCarthy Way

Los Angeles CA 90019

www.snhpr.com

ISBN: 978-1-7325543-2-0

CONTENTS

INTRODUCTION: WHAT IS MINIMALISM?	1
THE DISADVANTAGES OF THE PRESENT LIFESTYLE	5
THE ADVANTAGES OF MINIMALISM	11
TIPS FOR IMPLEMENTING MINIMALISM INTO YOUR LIFE	16
CONCLUSION	24

INTRODUCTION: WHAT IS MINIMALISM?

When thinking about minimalism, you may immediately think of the art or style that developed in the twentieth century but that is not what this book wants to address.

In this definition, minimalism literally means involving minimalized possessions. Think of the cliché of "less is more."

Minimalists choose to have fewer possessions, but those possessions mean a great deal to them. Many minimalists prefer this lifestyle because they believe what they have is of more value to them: they have more space and more money in their pockets. Many of them have reported not feeling stressed out and with a greater sense of self-worth and identity.

Minimalism may be confused with "de-consumption" which sounds like weight loss. De-consumption involves the idea of "We'd all be better off if we consumed less." This can mean consuming less food, using fewer items, and reducing things in your life in general. This is not the definition of minimalism and should not be confused with it.

Minimalism can easily be misunderstood by people who try to over simplify it or make it too complex. It's easy to think that someone who lives with so little and can't be accused of excess is a minimalist. It is when a person chooses to assess his or her life and come to realize that there are some things that wouldn't be missed if they were gone.

Minimalism isn't about suffering or a self-imposed seeking redemption through misery and pain. Minimalism's intent is to bring a practical clarity into your life. It is not meant to be a negative thing and can only become one if the person chooses to turn it so.

If you are curious about living a minimalist lifestyle, you may be stuck at just how to go about it. How you choose to start and go about your minimalist lifestyle is up to you as there is no right or wrong way to start. Each person's minimalist lifestyle will be different as we are all different. There are no right or wrong colors or foods. Most people prefer a certain color, family, fashion or style but that isn't the only way.

The reason people choose to go into the minimalist lifestyle is as varied as the people who live it. Some people choose the minimalist lifestyle due to spiritualism, religious reasons, wishing to go for the practical, or even because of economic reasons. There is no right or wrong way when choosing to live the minimalist lifestyle.

Becoming a minimalist won't always be easy; it requires patience and will power but it can be well worth it in the end.

The minimalist lifestyle may make you curious. You may also be wondering what disadvantages, if any, are there to this present lifestyle.

What are listed as potential disadvantages may not be disadvantages to *you*. That is okay, if you do not feel they are disadvantages but still wish to push forward. I do not wish to discourage you from it. It is my hope to help you in your path when choosing the minimalist lifestyle.

THE DISADVANTAGES OF THE PRESENT LIFESTYLE

In today's world, we live in a very instant gratification culture, and it's easy to get wrapped up in that lifestyle. Everything is thrown at us that bigger is better and more is better. We can get so caught up in this that we don't know our own heads from a hole in the ground.

The current lifestyle that we have at this time is quantity over quality, which can no longer be sustained given the fact that the reconstruction of the American lifestyle has already begun.

Because of the consumer lifestyle we live, we are forced to reside in a complex society where "more is better" instead of "less is more." Everyone is in search of the next big thing which makes us want more and more until it spirals out of control.

When we live this lifestyle, budgeting can be very difficult and stressful. It's even tougher when you're buying stuff that you don't need or are buying more of what you already have because you forgot you have it in the first place.

You may even be spending money on things that you don't use or even need. Why pay for that landline bill when you rarely or never use it? If you have a cellphone and use that for all your calls why keep the landline around? Why pay for Cable T.V. and Internet when you can watch T.V. shows over the internet.

The over-abundance and buying stuff that we don't really need can breed discontentment. Sometimes the more we have, the more we feel we need. This can be a never ending cycle: we get more, it becomes a clutter, we get stressed, and the cycle continues. Having a cluttered house often leads to stress which is bad for our bodies and minds.

Renting a storage unit can help with the clutter but it won't solve the problem. If you get a storage unit then you're spending a certain amount of money on monthly rent and this adds up to even more budget problems.

Having a lot of clutter in our homes lead to a wasteful lifestyle. When our refrigerators and freezers get cluttered, we forget what we have.

This can lead to us buying more of what we don't need, or the food goes bad. This forces us to throw food away and buy new food items. This leads to more waste of money, and the cycle continues.

Even if you do make thrifty decisions and live a thrifty lifestyle, it is still possible to obtain and hold on to a bunch of clutter that you really don't need.

If you have young children, it can also be easy to forget what clothes they have. Children are always growing and always need new clothes. Some clothes get put away in drawers or shoved into the back of the closet. When you eventually get some of these clothes out of the closet, you find out that the children have already outgrown them.

This lifestyle can make you feel like you're running a rat race or trying to "keep up with the Joneses". You can't win either way. Trying to, or even realizing that can be a hard and frustrating experience.

It's not fun having all of that wasted and negative energy going into this when you aren't getting anything in return.

When you have a great deal of stuff, it's easy to forget what is special and what is not. Those photographs and memories are special. Sentimental things are special but what about everything else? May be not so much.

All of these can add up to a living beyond your means sort of lifestyle. You may have to worry about where each paycheck is going to and how you will make ends meet. This can be incredibly stressful as bills and other things pile up around you.

What happens if and when you have to move to a new house or even downgrade to a smaller place? You'll be forced to go through a great deal of stuff in a short amount of time. This isn't an easy process, and it can become stressful as you may not know what to keep and what to throw out.

By having many items, we lose track of what is important and what is not. The things that are important to us at one point may become things that are lost in a sea of things at other times.

It can be tough to live the minimalist lifestyle if your heart isn't into it but it's even tougher to live the one that you already have if you're miserable and stressed out all the time. Living minimalist is a lifestyle adjustment and a permanent journey but it does have a great many advantages which leads us to…

THE ADVANTAGES OF MINIMALISM

These days, we live in a world of complexities which can make stripping them away very appealing to us. While minimalism may sound appealing, you may be wondering what the advantages of Minimalism are.

There are many advantages to living the minimalist lifestyle, some of which you may have not even thought of.

Did you know that it's hard to lose things? If you only own a certain amount of things, you're far more likely to *never* have a problem finding them! If you're not spending time searching for an elusive item, you are going to have more free time to do the activities and things that you enjoy.

If you ever have to move, moving all your stuff only takes a few hours, a day at most. If you're not moving too far, odds are very strong you can move all your items in just a few trips. If you're moving far away, think about just how quickly you can load and then unload a U-Haul truck.

You'll also have more money in your pocket. If you're not spending money on stuff or buying stuff you already have but forgot you have, you'd be saving a great deal. This saving can turn into investments which will help you make even more money.

You'll also have more free time if you don't need to buy as much stuff. You also won't need to work so many hours to pay for it. If there's a movie you want to see or a book you want to read, you can check it out from the library which also saves you money!

You may even achieve a greater sense of self when living the minimalist lifestyle.

People have reported getting *high* from buying things, or gaining confidence when shopping. If you break this addiction, then, you'll only have a few items and yourself. By doing this you'll have greater value in yourself rather than the items that you possess. In the end, the items are just "things", what matters is you and your sense of self.

Living the minimalist lifestyle means there will be less stuff that you have to clean. Wouldn't it be so much better to only have to clean a few items than a whole bunch of stuff?

Along with a greater sense of self, you may also feel a greater sense of inner peace. When you have less things to keep track of, your mind will relax and your stress levels will go down. Having lots of clutter around often increase stress and anxiety, so if you suffer from these conditions a minimalist lifestyle may be something to consider.

When you choose to adopt the minimalist lifestyle, you also find yourself jumping out of the rat race. Every time you think you get somewhere, they invent a better rat. Jumping out of the rat race will help you accept yourself for whom and what you are. Doing this will decrease your stress, even on a subconscious level, and help you achieve inner peace.

Everything on some level will matter and have value to you. Each item that you own will be something that you truly value and are grateful for. Having only five or six shirts will matter more to you than the twenty plus you had before. Everything you'd own will become important and something you're sure never to lose.

There will be far less waste for you to deal with and this will help you reduce your carbon footprint and there will be less trash entering our landfills.

If you have children introducing them to the minimalist lifestyle is a good way to introduce them to what's important and what isn't. It's a great way to teach children to value what they have and help give them good structure.

The minimalist lifestyle isn't permanent and it is always changing as you re-evaluate everything in your life. No two people will have the exact same minimalist lifestyle and that is normal and okay.

If you try the minimalist lifestyle and decide that it's not for you, you can always go back or learn ways to adapt it so that it becomes comfortable to you. The minimalist lifestyle, while strict, does not mean that you are confined to only *one* idea or way.

Are you ready to learn some handy tricks and tips to living a minimalist lifestyle? Read on below!

TIPS FOR IMPLEMENTING MINIMALISM INTO YOUR LIFE

Choosing to live the minimalism lifestyle is a lifestyle change and one that must be kept up often. Once you get started and become established in living your minimalist lifestyle, it will become easier to maintain.

If this sounds interesting to you but you're stuck on where to get started, try searching online for pictures of minimalist homes and lifestyles. This will help you get an idea of what you like and what you don't like.

One of the first things you need to do is introduce Multi-Purpose items (like clothing, transportation, electronics and kitchenware) into your lifestyle. By doing this first, you will be surprised how your lifestyle will shrink after this first process. This is a must if you want to live the minimalist lifestyle. Because of this, keeping a hold on your budget should not be too difficult.

For your budget, separate utilities, water, and medicines that are necessary for your life. After that, devise what other things you may need to maintain your minimalist lifestyle. Every once in a while, you will need new clothes, appliances, and other things. This is because what we have does wear out, break, and occasionally get lost. If you need this, spend the extra time to budget it in.

Another important thing is to de-clutter your stuff. Clutter is the enemy of a minimalist lifestyle and you cannot live with it. If you have a lot of clutter, start with one room or an area at a time rather than taking it all on at once. When you are done choosing what you need and don't need, you can hold a garage sale and/ or donate the items.

For bills, try having an area where you place them so your home cannot become littered with paper. Using a small basket that can be used for Car Keys/Bills will work well. If possible, consider going paperless when paying your bills. Many companies are choosing this option and it will save you the trouble of having papers in a certain area.

For any important papers and documentation, keep them all in one area and in a certain spot in your home. A Multi-Purpose cabinet will work very well for this as all of your papers will be in one area and easy to access.

Once you have sorted out your belongings and have a spot to place important information, rearrange your leftover possessions to make space. Having good space is a very important part of minimalism and without it things will get cluttered again. If you're having difficulty deciding how you want to rearrange your home, there are many sites and blogs online that can help you find an attractive and happy medium. Some sites will even help give you information on *Feng shui* which has become quite popular in the recent years.

If you like accent décor, try embellishing what you have or even buying a few pieces that you really like.

If you like neutral shades, try neutral shades in your house. Try choosing pieces that are in a similar color group.

You can stay organized by keeping electronics, DVDs and books out of sight and inside of multi- purpose storage cabinets. You can also enjoy free entertainment by going to your library and checking out books and movies.

Try to reduce yourself down to one item for each kind of task. Unless it is for something important you should only have one car, one phone, etc. If there's no practical reason to have multiples of these items, consider donating or selling them. There are companies out there that will take old phones and refurbish them to help people who are in dangerous situations. Maybe you know someone who could use that old car? You can donate it and receive a nice tax deduction in the process.

Take the time to evaluate your life and your needs. Some people don't need a car as they live near public transportation, can get rides from friends, or even walk everywhere.

As just about everyone has a cell phone do you need that landline? If you answered "no" then why not cancel it? Likewise if you have a landline do you need a cell phone?

Not everyone does and your needs will vary depending on it.

Along with clearing out what no longer serves you, it is also important to clean out your wardrobe. This may be a time consuming task as our wardrobe is a big part of who we are.

As everything in a minimalist lifestyle should serve a purpose, it is important to see what clothes you do and do not need. Unless they have sentimental value or are important for something you may want to consider donating them.

One of the first things to do is to decide what you must keep. These can include things of sentimental value; something important in your family, or something that has a positive memory.

After you have completed the first task of cleaning out your wardrobe, it's time to get serious. When sorting through your clothes put anything that doesn't fit or you don't like anymore into the pile first. Go through the remaining items and ask yourself how often do you use them? If you haven't used any of the items within a year, add them to the pile.

After you have decided what you wish to keep it is time to organize your wardrobe. There are many ways you can choose to organize the remainder of your wardrobe. If items are out of season you can place them in multipurpose boxes and place them somewhere safe. If you don't wish to box them you can hang them in your closet and organize them by item, color, type of clothing, or even shape. The only limit to how you choose to organize your clothing is your imagination.

They say every woman needs a "little black dress" and every man needs a "neck tie" but do you? Does your lifestyle require one? If you don't need it then donate it to your local GoodWill Store. Think about your daily activities, events, and social occasions and obligations when analyzing your wardrobe necessities.

This then leads us to the question: what should you purchase in clothing? We are all built differently so once you learn what type of body you have, you can look up information on what will work the best for you.

When choosing clothing, you must choose quality over quantity. Pay attention to labels and choose clothing that looks like it is good quality.

Many minimalists prefer neutral colors as they are easy to mix and match. The ability to do this will allow you to make multiple outfits which are a signature to a minimalist wardrobe. If you like color blocks, this is also something to consider.

CONCLUSION

The minimalist lifestyle is a constant work in progress as you evaluate and reevaluate what's important and necessary in your life. Think of it as a journey rather than a destination.

At first it may seem as hard, even rather difficult to achieve this lifestyle but once you take that first step of implementing Multi-Purpose into your Lifestyle, you are well on your way to achieving the minimalist lifestyle.

There are many reports and testimonials from people who have tried the minimalist lifestyle and have come to thoroughly enjoy it. In fact, many of them have reported feeling happier and better about themselves.

If you need help beginning and maintaining a minimalist lifestyle, there are many tips and tricks available online to help you with everything from finances to décor.

If you've considered a minimalist lifestyle now is a great time to start!